PURSUING MY WONDERFUL

By Beth Tancredi

Pursuing My Wonderful
©2017

Beth Tancredi

All rights reserved. No part of this book may be reproduced in any form without permission in writing from the author. Reviewers may quote brief passages in reviews.

Published February 15, 2017
ISBN: 978-0-9985710-0-3

DISCLAIMER No part of this publication may be reproduced or transmitted in any form or by any means, mechanical or electronic, including photocopying or recording, or by any information storage and retrieval system, or transmitted by email without permission in writing from the author.

Dedication

*For those women who long for something more, may
you always pursue your wonderful in life
(no matter how big or small).*

PREFACE

"When you realize you want to spend the rest of your life with somebody, you want the rest of your life to start as soon as possible."

– When Harry Met Sally

This quote has always had a special place in my heart – not just because that's what I have wanted in my Mr. Wonderful, but because I believe this is true of *any* wonderful in your life.

When you find it, you just want to *be* with it.

I have my Mr. Wonderful, but I have grown tired - tired of waiting for the rest of wonderful to appear and tired of looking in the wrong places and trying to make a corporate relationship work. I know in my heart that it's just not for me.

I have big ideas and have been flirting with a career shift for a while now, but I've been scared. I've been gripped by the fear that I'm simply not good enough to make those ideas work and I'm terrified of the impact it could have on me and my family if I make the wrong choices.

But it's time for me to take a risk and put myself out there, to start making the move from the full-time corporate world to starting my own business.

Oddly enough, pursuing my professional wonderful looks an awful lot like the steps I took in pursuing (and keeping) my Mr. Wonderful after being 'off the market' for a while.

And it doesn't start until you simply take the first step and put yourself out there.

Throughout this book, I will introduce you to women (and men) like us who have felt like there is more wonderful out there for them. They have taken a risk, put themselves out there and built a long-term relationship with their passion – and have even made money doing it!

After all, *"When you realize you want to spend the rest of your life doing something, you want the rest of your life to start as soon as possible."*

TABLE OF CONTENTS:

From the Author ix

Mentor Profile: Laura Virili 1

Chapter 1: Tired of Waiting for Wonderful................. 5

Mentor Profile: Kim Albano 15

Chapter 2: Putting Yourself Out There 17

Mentor Profile: Tom Paolella 29

Chapter 3: Building the Profile.................................. 31

Mentor Profile: Laine Crosby..................................... 50

Chapter 4: Frogs and Princes: Finding the
 Right Fit 53

Mentor Profile: Amy Brooks 58

Chapter 5: Committing: When It's Time for
 'The Conversation' 61

Mentor Profile: Mark Devenpeck.............................. 67

Chapter 6: Keeping the Passion Alive 71

Mentor Profile: Jaycee Gerard 80

Chapter 7: Surviving 'The Lovers' Quarrel' 83

Chapter 8: Pursue Your Wonderful........................... 91

Acknowledgements 97

About the Author... 101

From the Author

Once, as we were lamenting about not having a hobby or passion in life, my best friend said to me, "You have a passion that you probably never even realized you have. You like to learn about different businesses and careers and how people like them."

That sounded silly, but she was right.

Every single time I have felt the itch to shift careers, I have looked to my network of people around me (in person or on social media) and started asking questions. Lots of them.

In the early 2000s, I had my mind set on being a teacher. So, I hunted down every teacher I could think of to learn more about it. Local teachers. Out-of-state teachers. Public school teachers. Private school teachers. Tenured and non-tenured teachers. I even looked into purchasing a daycare franchise.

What did they like about their career? What didn't they like? What were the biggest obstacles they faced?

Was it fulfilling?

After all the conversations were done, I came to the conclusion that teaching kids was simply not my thing. So my research was worth it.

Since then, I have either formally or informally interviewed individuals in different industries and roles in a soul-searching effort to understand 'what I want to do when I grow up.'

Pursuing My Wonderful is the culmination of some of those conversations. It is the direction that I needed in order to find (and get to) where I belong professionally.

This book features insights from interviews with six people, my mentors if you will, who graciously offered their time to speak with me about how they went about pursuing their own wonderful and started their own businesses. They are my friends, my colleagues (past and present), and in some cases, simply network connections with whom I've built relationships over time.

MENTOR PROFILE: Laura Virili

Leading social media influencer, speaker, and private coach

LauraVirili.com

It's hard to believe that I have known Laura Virili for almost 20 years already. I met her in 1998 during my first stint in the financial services industry. No one needed to tell you that Laura was intelligent and self-assured – she simply exuded it. And she was hungry for something else in life. She just couldn't put her finger on it.

Not long after we started working together, she moved on to another firm. And by my one-year anniversary in financial services, she had taken me right along with her.

If I had a dollar for every time we sat down and talked about the 'something more' that was out for us, well, I'd have been well-funded to start pursuing my wonderful much earlier than I did.

We worked together when she got married. And we worked together when I got engaged. She was even at my wedding.

But as times and career changes happen, Laura and I drifted apart, connected only by a network connection on LinkedIn and a profile on Facebook.

My curiosity was piqued, though, when I started seeing social media notifications that, after serving many more years in financial services, Laura made her big, bold professional move away from the corporate life and moved on to pursuing her wonderful on her own.

After spending years in financial services, Laura realized she had the intelligence, the background and the presence to take her knowledge on the road.

She now helps people find their personal brand and tell their story by coaching financial advisors and other professionals on the social selling process. And she does it exactly where she belongs – on the stage.

While she does offer one-on-one training and coaching, she spends most of her time traveling the country speaking to hundreds (and even thousands) about how they can use social media to drive their business results.

CHAPTER 1

Tired of Waiting for Wonderful

My eyes spring open. It's 4:45 a.m., fifteen minutes before my alarm is set to go off. I'm jarred awake, sweating, just thinking about the impending day at work. I try to close my eyes to squeeze in the extra fifteen.

It's no use. I'm up.

I get up and brush my teeth while the shower water warms up.

Beep. Beep. Beep.

I hear my alarm outside the bathroom. "Damn," I think to myself, "I never shut it off. I hope it doesn't wake the kids." But I'm in no rush to run to my bedroom and turn it off either.

I get out of the shower and scrounge around my dark room for clothes. I would turn the lights on, but my youngest son has been sleeping in my room because he tore a ligament in his leg and can't climb up into his loft bed. He's not a kind sleeping partner, but I still try to be considerate given why he's in my room.

I throw on my standard uniform – jeans and a t-shirt. There was a time when I dressed to impress to go into work, but I can't be bothered with that anymore given the hour and my lack of interest in primping. I'd rather be comfortable anyway.

At 5:35 a.m., I sit down at what was once my grandparents' cherry dining room table (now scratched up and weathered from almost 14 years with kids) to start my workday from home. I do a quick assessment of what I can get done before my older son's alarm goes off at 6:00 a.m.

The work is mundane and tedious, but it is the lifeblood of my company so it requires laser-focus. The only things to distract me at this hour are the quiet chatter of the 5:00 news and my faithful cat who takes her position in my lap.

Pull the data. Organize it. Process it. Make it pretty. Repeat.

Beep! Beep! Beep!

My son's alarm is screaming from upstairs. I let it go for a minute as I determine whether I'm at a good halting point and whether or not he's stirring.

He's not.

I head up the stairs to get him.

"It's time to get up, buddy," I say as my usual mantra for him at that hour.

"Noooo. I can't," he responds.

"You can."

"No."

"I'm turning on the light."

"Nooooooo…." He begs. "Hold on," he says, cocooning himself in his comforter to block out the light.

"You have to get up," I plead, "I have a ton of work this morning and I don't have time to keep coming back up here. Promise me."

"Okay," groans the lump in the bed.

"Are you sure?"

"Mm-hmm."

I plod back down to my laptop, dimly lit by the overhead lamp, and the now 6:00 news.

It's still quiet upstairs. "Nick!" I yell, "Get up!"

"I AM!" says an angry voice as my focus returns to my screen.

"What the…???"

The data. Something's wrong with the data. I can feel myself growing flushed.

"You've got this," I breathe. "Go back and start over. It will be fine."

But my access to the original data has been denied. And no matter how many times my trembling fingers make the attempt, I just can't get in.

I play around with alternative solutions and with every attempt, failure – not because the solutions aren't good ones, but because I'm so flustered that every fix breaks something else. I shove the laptop away from me, attempting to admit defeat.

It is just the first time today that I will want to crawl under the table, curl up in a ball and cry.

Defeat isn't an option though. There is no one but me

to fix this problem – at least not in time for our impending morning deadlines.

"Mom, don't we have to get to the bus?"

I look at the time again. 6:25 a.m.

"Shit," I mutter under my breath as I grab my car keys, leaving my laptop open to sit and think about what it's done.

We get to the bus stop and with a few minutes to spare before the bus arrives, we sit in the car while Nick quietly watches his mother teetering on the edge of a nervous breakdown.

At 6:31, I kick him out of the car but stay until the bus arrives.

I head back home dreading the next round with my laptop. As it turns out, the break is exactly what I needed. After a few more attempts, I finally get it and can finish the work I started an hour ago.

My problem has been resolved, but I can't say as much for the knot in my stomach or for my well-planned morning routine.

I'm hustling around the house to make sure my youngest gets up, gets dressed and his lunch (and mine) gets made. He sees my panic and, for once, takes some initiative to do what he can himself.

Somehow, I finish everything I need to do in the nick of time. I summon my youngest, grab my car keys and run out the door to get him off to school and me off to work.

Twenty-five minutes later, I park my car a block from my office and try to collect myself for a moment as I contemplate whether going home is an option.

Up until two years ago, I loved this job. No, it wasn't my passion, but it was my 'wonderful.' I gushed (to the point of embarrassment) to my friends and family about how much I loved coming into my job every day.

Don't get me wrong. I still love my job and the people I work with. I'm just not *in love* with it anymore.

My motto has long been, "Do what you love. Love what you do," and I REALLY want that back. But I won't find it here. Believe me, I've looked. I can't just dredge my old passion back up.

But how – or where – do I find that?

I get into my office, throw my lunch in the fridge and sit down to continue even more of what I was struggling with before I left the house.

Pull the data. Organize it. Process it. Make it pretty. Repeat.

The number crunching is making me nuts – as it would for anyone whose brain favors creativity.

I drift off momentarily to a conversation I had with my former colleague, Laura Virili, who now runs her own business as a social media influencer, speaker, and private coach. "Why aren't you writing anymore?" Laura asked me once. "You are one of the best writers I know. You need to start writing again."

"She's right," I whisper to myself. "Why am I not writing anymore? I loved writing."

I wrote my first book – a children's book – in the third grade as part of a class assignment. My book, entitled *A Pet for Me*, was about my pet gerbil and won me a trip to a Young Authors Convention. It was *the* thing that opened me up to a love of writing. (My mother still lights up whenever *A Pet for Me* is mentioned as if it was one of the all-time greats of children's books.)

I spent the years following writing a lot of poetry and personal essays. I wrote for me, rarely showing it to others because it let people into a side of me that I was just not quite ready to share. But man, did it feel good to just let it out, like a deep breath releasing the stress of anything and everything that was bothering me.

My office phone rings, snapping me back to my deadline-driven reality. I ignore it and let it find its way to voice mail.

No voice mail.

A moment later, it rings again. Same number on the caller ID. I let it go to voice mail again, but still no message.

Another few moments pass – guess who? Same number.

I ignore it once again, but this time they leave a message.

"You suck! Who do you think you are releasing numbers like that? You people are idiots!" I skip to the end and delete it.

No wonder I don't answer the phone anymore.

I haven't even realized how much time has gone by.

At 12:45 p.m., my mobile lights up. It's my youngest calling me on Facetime. He's just gotten off the bus because school was only a half day today.

"Mommy? I thought you said you were going to be home," he says sadly.

"I'm sorry, Christian. I was trying to finish up so I could work from home, but things have been crazy. I can't leave yet," I explained. "I'm so sorry."

"I know," he replied, "Then I will let you get back to work so you can finish up and get home as soon as possible."

"I'll do my best," I tell him, knowing full well that leaving the office even before 4:00 p.m. is a fantasy at this point.

I put my head on my desk, letting Christian's intense disappointment settle into my soul. "I can't keep doing this," I think to myself. "I should be home."

I have failed as a mother.

Tomorrow will be more of the same -- and I'm tired of these tomorrows.

Maybe it's just time to consider ending this relationship and finding one that truly meets my needs. But what are the pros and cons of staying versus going?

Staying	Going
Pros:	**Pros:**
- Love my coworkers - Love Asbury Park and that it's local - Positive daily challenges - At the top of the company - Decent salary - Somewhat flexible schedule	- Can find or create a role that is more amenable to my interests - Better salary - Financial stability? - Less stress? - No work on weekends or holidays
Cons:	**Cons:**
- Financial instability of the company - Weekend/holiday working hours - The role is more operations and data oriented	- Difficult to find a local job, may have to commute - Starting over - Corporate structure is no longer for me

MENTOR PROFILE: Kim Albano

Founder, Kicking Ass & Looking Pretty

KickingAssAndLookingPretty.com

My relationship with Kim Albano is a true example of how powerful your professional and social networks can be.

In 2016, Laura introduced me to Kim, a learning and development expert who had recently left the financial services world and was on the verge of launching her own personal and professional development business called Kicking Ass & Looking Pretty. At the time that we were introduced (virtually), Kim was looking for writers to contribute to a question and answer segment of her website across different fields of expertise and needed someone to write about life as a single mom.

And there I was. Writer. Single mom.

Since then, Kim and I have acted as a sounding board for one another, bouncing around different thoughts and ideas about women's issues and professional development. We've also offered support and encouragement in continuing to pursue our passions.

Kicking Ass & Looking Pretty was built to empower women to build or grow their businesses by generating new, fresh and unique ideas.

She offers one-on-one coaching, but has also built a community of amazing women who share their ideas and opportunities through an online learning platform called the K.A.L.P. Academy. She has more than 1,500 followers on Facebook.

CHAPTER 2

Putting Yourself Out There

"Every day, I expect at least one 'Wow' – I look for it and I get it!"

– Laura Virili, LauraVirili.com

I want the 'Wow.'

This is not the first time I have flirted with the idea of starting over. In fact, I have caught myself many, many times before sneaking a peek at what else is out there. My iPhone alerts me daily when it finds a good match – that special something that meets my needs, but I always find flaws.

I have too many years of experience. Too few years. Travel required. Missing key qualifications in one area, but have too many in another. Geographically undesirable.

I also realize that I've been secretly hoping that someday my wonderful would just be bestowed upon me 'when I least expect it.'

So far, all that has done is leave me with tightly closed eyes chanting, "I'm not expecting it *now!*" under my breath.

"You should have your resume out there," my friends and family often say. But that's not what I want or need.

I don't need another 9-5 (or in my case 6-4ish) job that carries over into the evenings and weekends and has me working through holidays.

Call me picky, but my wonderful doesn't look like that.

So, what does it look like? I realize that I will have to be flexible on some things, but I'm not willing to sacrifice others.

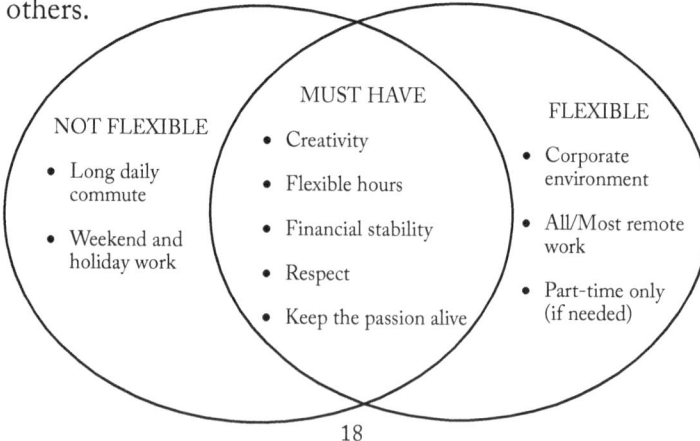

One thing is clear – I can no longer *wait* for wonderful. I'm going to have to find it some other way. And I'm not going to settle for less, even if it means kissing a few frogs along the way.

> ***"I have never once gotten up and dreaded going into work – I love it all."***
>
> – Jaycee Gerard, JayceeGerardPhoto.com

My mind wanders off as I fantasize about what *that* looks like – loving what I do with my life again so much that I don't dread working for even one day.

The thoughts dance behind my eyes, teasing me with the different directions I can go. And then I see it through the fog. My muse is summoning me from the across the room, gesturing for me to follow because it knows *exactly* what I need. Even though I can't quite put my finger on it myself.

It's exhausting and thrilling all at once. To be wanted. To know that there's a better fit out there for me. To feel something in my stomach that is, for the first time in a while, not the feeling of a growing ulcer but more like butterflies.

Similar to my friends who had "the perfect guy" for me after my divorce, my muse may know what's right for me, but I'm still trying to put it together.

It may seem silly or maybe even unrealistic, but I really just want to find joy in what I'm doing and how I'm spending my time.

"When choosing your path, it is important to do what you love. But it is equally important that it's something you're good at."

– Mark Devenpeck, TriadYogaCa.com

But how do you define that?

There are plenty of things I love to do. There are plenty of things I'm good at. But where is the intersection that combines both?

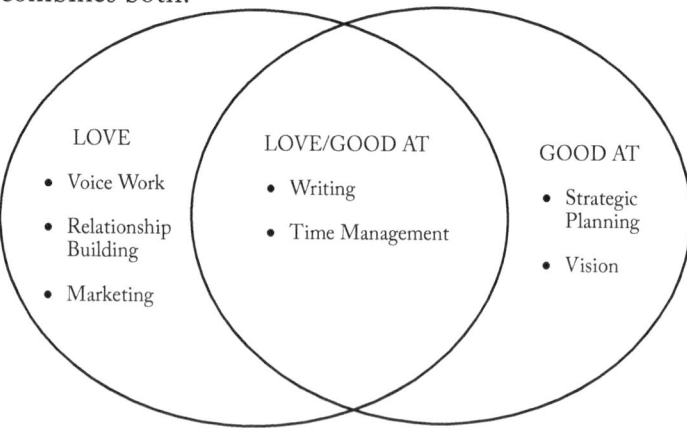

That intersection in the middle is where I need to be. The sweet spot. That's not to say that I can't work the other pieces that I love or that I'm good at into my wonderful. Those can be nothing but beneficial in my journey forward with wonderful.

Amy Brooks expanded on Mark's thoughts a bit further.

"Ask yourself three questions: Am I good at this? Do I like it? Who will pay me for it?"

– Amy Brooks, VoicePenPurpose.com

She's right. You may be spiritually rewarded by following your passion, but the pursuit of your professional wonderful will really only be successful as a business if someone is paying you to do it.

I remember during the first interview for the job I have now, the company's founder asked me whether I thought of myself as a creative person or a numbers person. And clear as day, I remember answering him with the words, "I have always thought of myself as a creative person, but I have come to find that numbers paint their own pictures and tell their own stories as well. So, I would say I am both."

That was only partly true, of course, because my passion is truly ignited when I am not looking at numbers, but I would say it's the thing that got me the job in the first place.

To me, painting a picture through narrative *feels* better than painting by numbers.

And suddenly I can see it more clearly than I've ever seen it before. I want to be an author – a voice. For me. For others.

Just thinking about that word – author – feels just so warm and cozy. It feels like home.

I love the creativity of putting the pieces of an informational puzzle together to create one big picture. It's always a challenge. Do you start from the edges and work your way in, or work on the inside first?

In my heart, I know I can make something of it. And it makes me question what ever made me put down my pen in the first place.

Perhaps it was my fear of being a 'starving artist,' that directed me away from writing and into marketing-related roles. Perhaps I was afraid I just wouldn't stand out

– after all, there are plenty of people out there who have what I can offer – why would anyone choose me?

I traded my creativity for logistics and operations years ago and it's taken its toll.

I mean, let's face it, I'm not the same person I was in my 20s and 30s. My face is a bit more weathered, wrinkled from years of staring at computer screens and a furrowed brow from, well, doing it all on my own. My brain is a bit more analytical, more calculating.

Plenty of people I know have put themselves out there to follow their passion and find wonderful. There's no reason I can't do the same.

But I'm a 'by the book' type of woman who is struggling to make a decision between the work that feeds my soul and the one that feeds my kids.

Thinking about leaving what I have feels a bit irresponsible – who am I kidding? It feels VERY irresponsible. I'm a single mother who relies on a steady income. I have stability in a full-time job and this job is really far more flexible than most full-time jobs out there. And it's local. That's a big deal.

In my case, it might make more sense to start small.

> ***"Following your 'crazy idea' or your passion really depends on your current state in life. If you're going all in, have a plan B in mind in case this one doesn't work out. If you don't, make it a calculated risk."***
>
> – Tom Paolella, CarConciergePlus.com

I don't have a plan B. For me, the calculated risk is the smarter approach. So maybe the right step is to put myself out there slowly. Test the waters. Be smart about it. It may take years to fully cut my ties with my full-time job, but I would be doing so without risking the security of me and the boys.

The good news is, I'm not talking about an investment here other than my time. Although it's a commodity, it's the less risky option than going all in.

However, in starting up a part-time business, I have to remember that my full-time job is the one that pays the bills and, for that reason, it still deserves 100% of my effort. Therefore, my new job can only be done during my time outside of normal business hours. That's a balancing act that I will need to work out with my children and it cannot interfere with my ability to be a good mother.

I should also caution that before making any decisions on taking a part-time approach, you should check your employee regulations about outside work and non-compete issues if applicable.

With a rough plan to start small in mind combined with Laura's inspirational words to get me back on the writing track, I am starting to believe that letting the writer inside of me out would undoubtedly lead to good things in my life.

"Books are the new business card."

– Laura Virili

When Laura first encouraged me to write a book, I didn't realize that blogging held similar value.

And I actually started it months ago without even trying to when I started blogging as a creative outlet to my professional life in operations.

In fact, it was less than a month after I started blogging that former colleagues who are friends of mine on Facebook started taking notice and asking if I would ever consider freelance work.

Some of those conversations did not lead to business opportunities, but some did. And the ones that didn't, just didn't work out *at the time*. Those doors are still open.

They say the first step is often the hardest – and sometimes that step is just making the decision to put yourself out there.

If that's the case, the good news is I can check that box off already.

For you, getting yourself out there may look a little different. As you're contemplating whether or not to pursue your wonderful, Kim Albano suggests having *intentional* conversations about your passion to help put the pieces together.

> *"Pay close attention to what people are asking for. Have intentional conversations and then figure out how to apply your business to what people need. If you don't know what people need, you will be off the mark."*
>
> – Kim Albano

Intentional conversations not only serve to help *you* fill in the gaps of what it is *you're* looking for, but they also subtly let people around you know what you are passionate about so they will think about you the next time it comes up.

Mark Devenpeck's business, Triad Yoga & Pilates, for example, discovered an untapped market for their business simply by listening to what their clients wanted. The suggestion? They should start teaching classes at some of the major apartment complexes in the area.

And with a little persistence, Triad Yoga and Pilates made their way 'in' not just to the one complex his clients were requesting, but to a number of complexes run by the same management company.

Being the 'new kids on the block' at that time, it was the turning point they needed to build their name within the community.

I looked for similar 'untapped markets' when I was ready to start dating again after my divorce. "I think I'm ready," I'd say to close friends. "If you know of anyone who might have some things in common with me, I'd love to talk to them."

Even when I went on actual dates, intentional conversations served two purposes for me:

1- Learn enough about the other person to know if I wanted to go on a second (or third or fourth) date with him.
2- Look internally at how I presented myself – was I comfortable? Was I being true to myself?

Dating, as it turned out, was actually like interviewing for a job (and also like starting your own business). It's a two-way conversation to make sure it's a good fit for everyone, AND you only get better at it with more practice!

But is the introduction of wonderful to yourself and others enough to turn it into a business that can sustain the lifestyle you've become accustomed to?

This is what I lose sleep over.

A braver soul than I would say that anything is possible if you put your mind to it and that if you believe in what you're doing and commit to it, only positive things can come of it. But the reality is that it's not always that simple.

It takes thought. It takes planning. It takes commitment. And most of all, it takes work.

MENTOR PROFILE: Tom Paolella
Founder, Car Concierge Plus, LLC
CarConciergePlus.com

In 2009, Tom was hired by a local health care system where I worked to manage public relations for one of our hospitals. Although our paths did not often cross in our day-to-day work, you couldn't miss his passion for PR and the health care industry as a whole. As a matter of fact, you couldn't miss his passion for *anything* that he enjoyed – music, fine food and cars to name a few.

In 2013, three years after I left the health care industry, Tom moved on to a senior communications position at a global leader in protection solutions that manufactures protective industrial and medical gloves, clothing, and condoms and is tackling that position with the same glowing pride that he had when I worked with him.

But the one passion Tom could never put aside was his love of cars.

I remember, in fact, that while working at the health care system, his knowledge of cars so impressed members of the local Rotary Club that they offered him part-time work at their dealership. That experience, although short-lived, offered him behind-the-scenes knowledge of the car business.

And that experience turned out to be invaluable.

After driving (pun intended) that car-shopping experience for his cousin, it took a mere eight words for Tom to realize it was time to pursue his passion:

"I would have paid you to do that."

With that, Car Concierge Plus, LLC was born as a part-time venture for Tom to offer end-to-end car- buying services for anyone country-wide who does not want to go through the hassle and frustration of buying a car.

By July 4th of 2013, he had his first paying client. By the end of year three, Tom had amassed over 180 clients, including more than 50 who have now used his services more than once – a figure he proudly touts (and should).

And by the way, as of July 2016, I also became one of his clients and a huge advocate of his services.

CHAPTER 3

Building the Profile

"If you're passionate about something, you can find a way to make it work. Sometimes people just need a kick in the ass to get them to do it. After that, it's accountability."

- Kim Albano

Take a moment to think about that word – accountability.

As a single mom, I am accountable not just to myself but to my children. They need me to be able to continue to support them both emotionally and financially.

It's a heavy weight to bear.

Even now, providing that kind of support can be incredibly overwhelming. After a tough day of work, it's not unlike me to come home and flip out on my children over a bag thrown haphazardly in the middle of the floor.

Can you imagine how I will be when I'm strapped for cash as I go on my pursuit of my wonderful? Or if I've taken a wrong turn in that pursuit?

So, as I look for wonderful I need to be true to myself and true to my children by setting reasonable goals with reasonable expectations. In return, my wonderful needs to be understanding about my lifestyle and priorities.

Ever tried online dating? You may start to see the parallels.

How?

1- It's risky! You are attempting to connect to something that (or someone who) is unfamiliar to you.

2- Qualities of wonderful. You need to have an idea of the qualities you are looking for and be realistic about your expectations.

3- The competitive edge. You need to know what your competition is doing so you can differentiate yourself.

4- Sell it! You need to sell yourself.

5- See it through! You need to be confident enough in yourself to see it through, even if it doesn't work out the first time.
6- Expose yourself! You need to expose yourself to the experience as much as possible to get the most out of it.
7- And the most eerily similar - you're so excited about the opportunity that your heart beats rapidly when you think about it and you lose sleep over it.

It's Risky!

No matter how you look at it, connecting with strangers has its inherent risks. And when I was dating, I didn't want to waste my time trying to be something I wasn't or connect with someone who didn't share my interests.

I also wanted to make sure I wasn't in any danger.

My best friend, who was also recently divorced and online dating at the same time, and I are fiercely protective of one another.

Our requirements for any blind date were: Whom will you be with, what is his number, where are you going, text me when you get there and text me when you get home.

Throughout the evening, we also required text check-ins. I'm not talking about the fake emergency call (oh c'mon, don't act like you never had a friend do that for you!) I'm talking about a text with safe words. Only the two of us knew how to use those code words and fortunately for both of us, we never had to use the unsafe code.

In pursuing my professional wonderful, I am also going to need to take some risks.

> ***"I don't always know if something's going to work, but I'll still try it. If you can't take some creative risks, you're never going to progress."***
>
> *– Jaycee Gerard*

But reducing that risk means having safe words of a different sort. My safe words are boundaries that I have identified – the outer limit that I am willing to go to without jeopardizing my own principles, needs or ideas at this stage of my life.

Years later, my safe and unsafe codes are still just for me and my best friend to know, but I'm happy to share my boundaries when it comes to my professional wonderful:

- Does not force me outside of my comfort zone in terms of hours worked.
- Never puts me in a situation in which I have to make decisions that push my ethical limits.
- Does not belittle me, or make me feel like any less of an intelligent person for having different opinions.
- Does not require me to sacrifice a comfortable life for me and my kids.

It's funny… until now, my professional limits seemed too lofty and unrealistic to me. Now that I've written them down, though, they truly reveal themselves as both realistic and achievable – and I've certainly earned the right to all of them.

Qualities of Wonderful

From Chapter 2, I already know my must-haves and I know there are things that I will need to be flexible on. The same was true when I was venturing into the dating world.

Rock climbers, guys who travel out of the country on a whim or party animals need not apply.

Sometimes I could tell right away that it simply wasn't a good fit.

One night, I met a guy – we'll call him George, because it was so long ago that I honestly don't even remember his name – at Applebees for drinks. He seemed nice enough. We sat for hours talking and learning about one another. He was handsome enough, but I really wasn't in it for the looks.

Occasionally, he'd want to step outside for a cigarette and a make-out session. Seriously, first date! Okay, that's fine. Nothing I couldn't handle.

At one point, we went back into the restaurant to resume our conversation. And then it happened: "My mother cooks dinner for me and the kids every night. She cleans the house for us, too. I don't have to do anything. I really like that in a woman."

Annnnd that was the last time I spoke with him.

Similarly, I'm not looking for another job in which I am responsible for absolutely everything. I want to be a writer and editor, not all things to all people. And certainly not a number cruncher.

Other times, I gave a new relationship a month (or a few) to truly feel it out and see if it was something I could make work.

The first person I seriously dated after my divorce was actually someone whom I had seen on an online dating site but was 'geographically undesirable' in my mind. One night, I ended up at the bar where my best friend works because she had torn her contact lens and needed me to bring her glasses to her.

"Just stick around at the bar," she said. "There's a comedy show, so you can sit and watch."

I awkwardly sat at the corner of the bar, having a drink or two and laughing at the mediocre comedy. And there on the opposite side of the bar was one of the most handsome men I'd ever seen. His eyes sparkled even in the dimly lit bar and I didn't recognize him as the geographically undesirable person I had seen online.

I kept stealing glances.

"See that guy on the other side of the bar?" I asked my best friend. "Do you know him? He's really cute."

He wasn't one of the regulars, so I just let it be. And then he disappeared.

The comedy show wrapped up and suddenly that very same man sidled up next to me at the bar and bought me a drink. "My friends are getting ready to leave, so I have to go. But I didn't want to leave without introducing myself because I couldn't help but notice your smile."

He talked to me for all of about two minutes, gave me his number and asked me to call. The interaction was so quick that the people I knew who were working at the bar referred to him as "speed date" from there on out.

"Speed date" lasted six months, but after a while it became clear that he was more interested in drinking and going out with friends than I cared to do or had time to offer. So I ended it.

Perhaps you've seen job listings like this… ones that talk about the incredible social atmosphere with frequent gatherings for drinks after work. I'm an adult now. A single mother. While this certainly had its appeal in my 20s, it most definitely does not hold any appeal now. I often adore my coworkers, but I already spend more time with them than I do with my kids. This is not my wonderful either.

Why am I telling you this?

My wonderful respects my career, my family and shares in the responsibilities. As should yours – whether it's a relationship with a person or a relationship with your professional passion.

I'm also telling you this because it's okay to reset your priorities on both once you get involved as well.

The Competitive Edge

"It's a noisy, noisy world. But you never know when something will resonate with someone where it hasn't before."

– Laura Virili

Whether it always feels like it or not, you have a lot to bring to the table when it comes to pursuing your wonderful. Sure, others may be providing the same products and services or talking about the same things, but it takes just one word, one offering, one experience to differentiate yourself from everyone else out there and stand out. You need to break through the clutter.

And you can.

Now you may think this is weird, but when I did get up the courage to set up an online dating profile, I first snuck a peek at what people were saying in their profiles – and yes, I looked at both men AND women.

Why?

Because you need to know what the competition is doing and how you can do it better – especially if, like me, you're creating a business that so many other people are already doing.

In online dating, I felt it was important to get to know how people presented themselves. What were men looking for? And more importantly, what were women saying about themselves? I learned from both.

What kind of pictures were people posting? What were their interests? How were the profiles written – chock-full of detail or short and to the point? Well-written or slapped together? What were their usernames - cute and clever or simply their name?

As I was doing my research, I took note of the things that turned me off and things that interested me. I took the time to figure out not just how I wanted to sell myself, but what would be of interest when I looked at profiles of prospective dates.

In essence, the exercise helped me position myself for success in love (cheesy, I know), similar to the way that my must haves/must not haves list helped me identify my end-goals for my business or the next phase of my professional life.

Sell It!

In the pursuit of my passion to be that go-to writer or editor, what could I say or do that would differentiate myself from others and resonate with people in a way that others haven't been able to do before?

- Having worked in a number of industries, including financial services, health care, print and digital media, I have professional knowledge and experience to speak to different topics in appropriate tones.
- I am relatable and my words reflect that.
- I am a storyteller with the ability to touch souls.
- I am the consummate professional in time management.

- I have an expansive network to bring in different resources and research if necessary.

These are the points that not only give me my competitive edge, but will help me hone in on whom I target and how I will sell my services to people.

Your list will likely look a bit different.

Are there things that your potential competition is (or isn't) doing that you can do better? The beauty of social media is that you can identify not just where *you* think there are areas for improvement in this type of business, but you can quietly observe and listen to what others are both praising and complaining about.

But remember, selling it means more than just differentiating yourself. To truly get noticed, you have to hustle.

> *"The hustle does wonders. It will get you everywhere."*
>
> – Laura Virili

Once you recognize what makes you different, go hustle!

Expose Yourself!

"It's critical that when something interests you, expose yourself to as much of it as possible. Get the view from all sides."

– Kim Albano

As with dating, the chances of finding wonderful are unlikely to happen your first time out of the gate. Trust me, I know. From setups to online dating, I went out on countless dates with countless people who were foreign to me.

I took a break from it when it got to the point of exhaustion. And believe me, it gets exhausting!

It's like going on job interviews over and over and over again.

How many different ways could I possibly tell the same story? How many more questions could I come up with to help me determine whether I had found the right fit? How many outfits did I have to put together so I could 'dress to impress?' Half of the time it was hard to keep it all straight!

"Can you remind me whom I am meeting tonight?" I once had to ask my best friend.

But ultimately, I was 'getting the view from all sides.'

I also learned right away that exposing myself to the experience didn't mean that I was registered to all online dating sites at once. For one thing, if I found someone on one site, I was likely to find him on another as well.

It was also just as easy to try one dating channel out at a time to see what worked. If one wasn't working for me after a few months, I looked at other options or I would return to my personal dating sources – friends and family. But no matter what path I took, I had to be present in that space.

In pursuing your professional wonderful, it's much the same.

> *"If you want to dominate in a space, you absolutely can. But you have to be present."*
>
> – Laura Virili

You will want to cast a net wide enough to begin identifying what it is you want, the type of clients you'd like to work with and where you want to be. What is it that makes your heart flutter when thinking about your passion and how can you turn that into something you can sell – whether it's a product or a service?

As time goes on, your targets for wonderful may get wider to include more products or services, or more focused as you discover your comfort level with different audiences.

> *"My initial mission started out simply as, 'I would like to attract people who need me and want to work with me to write their first book.' But as time went on, I added, 'and who are able to joyfully pay.' And most recently, 'and are women.'"*
>
> – Amy Brooks

And remember, if those plans don't work out, there are other fish in the sea.

See It Through!

> *"One mistake people make in launching an idea or a business is that people think they have to keep it a secret. Don't be afraid to tell people what you want to do. We don't spend enough time telling people about ideas."*
>
> – Kim Albano

Seeing it through has been one of my biggest challenges. Sometimes it's because I keep my ideas to myself, afraid of what others will say. Other times, I just don't believe I have the skills or the wherewithal to pull it off.

I'm full of ideas and probably could have been a millionaire already if I had just followed through with one or two of them. It's just so easy, though, to get distracted and deterred from your path by the naysayers – and admittedly, I am one of my own naysayers.

Case in point… In the late 90s and early 2000s, I commuted to and from New York City every day. The commute was about three hours a day in total. And on snowy days, it was the absolute worst to come back to my car in the train parking lot covered with snow and freezing. Sometimes my then-husband would go to clean it off before I got there, but other days that wasn't possible.

They say that necessity is the mother of invention. And so, my idea was to create a way for me to call my car from my cell phone and trigger a remote start from the train.

Keep in mind, these were the days well before smart phones and the modern technology that we enjoy today. And I just didn't have the connections or wherewithal to figure out how to make something like that work.

The idea was great in my mind, but well ahead of its time. Because wouldn't you know that I now drive a car that allows me to start it from anywhere through a mobile app!

I have had many ideas like this throughout my life and there was always someone blocking the way, saying it wasn't possible or was quick to point out the downside and the risks of trying them out. It's very easy to get caught up in that negativity.

Even writing this book, I have had my moments of doubt. My moments of 'this works for me, but why would it work for anyone else?'

That's putting it mildly. I have had days in which I sit at my laptop cursing at myself over my inability to write a single sentence and questioning why I ever thought I could pull off writing a book for myself, let alone for anyone else.

Pursuing wonderful is, no doubt, a journey full of obstacles and naysayers. But the more we sing it out, the more we can identify the *direction* for our passion – and 'stop' is not a direction.

If I stopped dating every guy I have vented to my friends and family about and they supported me with words like, "I don't know how you put up with that. Maybe you should put an end to it," I would have lost some quality experiences with some quality (but maybe not the right fit) men. And I most certainly would have given up on this whole dating thing long before I found the relationship I'm currently in.

For Laine Crosby, author, deciding to see her passion through required three things:

1. Awakening
2. Accepting
3. Surrendering

Awaken to what it is you want (or are called) to do. Accept your calling. Surrender (commit) to that calling – regardless of what others may think of it.

> *"A lot of people thought I was crazy. I knew I wasn't. But I had a network of people who DID support me. Concentrate on those who believe in what you're doing.*
>
> – Laine Crosby, LaineCrosby.com

So give yourself a chance. Expose your plan to others and let them provide encouragement – even if that encouragement means you need to make small shifts in your strategy.

(And seriously, if I can tell people I'm writing a book on something as far-fetched as a comparison between post-divorce dating and turning your passion into a business, I think you can proudly share your ideas as well!)

MENTOR PROFILE: Laine Crosby
New York Times best-selling author
LaineCrosby.com

My first full-time job out of college was with a leading cable network. It was during the time when using the internet as a means of marketing and sharing information was really just coming into its own as a communications vehicle. The department started out small, but the owners of the company saw the potential and started growing that part of the organization at a rapid pace. That is when I met Laine Crosby.

Laine joined our team as a New Media Marketing Director. A southern girl at heart, this intelligent, tall redheaded woman and talented writer had the kindest demeanor you'd ever want as a friend and on your team.

During our time at the network, our large department held regular offsite team-building meetings. At one such meeting, we were instructed to go around the room and tell one thing that no one knew about us. To this day, I can't remember what I told the group, but I remember what Laine told us.

"Growing up, my family traveled to different states to explore cemeteries and make rubbings of the tombstones," Laine explained.

This was a far cry from the family vacations I had taken as a child, so it seemed strange and fascinating at the same time. But being the daughter of an historian in an age well before the Ancestry.coms of the world existed, this was one of the ways you tracked people and their roots.

Laine and I lost touch after I moved back to New Jersey in 1997, but were brought back together by the joys of Facebook.

In 2013, I started seeing posts promoting her first book, *Investigative Medium - The Awakening*, about her own true story of moving to an 18th-century Maryland plantation and awakening to find herself suddenly psychic.

Shortly after it released, her book rose to the ranks of New York Times Best Seller. Look for a sequel to *Investigative Medium – The Awakening* at the end of 2017.

Though she still works full-time at a trade association for the banking industry, she has turned her passion (or in this case, her calling) into professional opportunity. In her spare time, she works with law enforcement, forensic scientists, detectives, missing persons networks, historians and archaeologists to find out what history has not revealed.

You may have seen Laine on the Travel Channel's *Mysterious Journeys* series, and *My Ghost Story* on the Biography Channel. She has been featured in the *Washington Post*, *San Francisco Chronicle* and numerous other local and national papers, radio shows, news and local television segments. You can also find Laine's work included in Detective Lee Loftlan's true crime anthology, as well as Historian Mark Nesbitt's last eight titles, and other books and blogs by authors including Forensic Psychologist Dr. Katherine Ramsland.

CHAPTER 4

Frogs and Princes: Finding the Right Fit

As I mentioned in Chapter 2, pursuing your passion may mean kissing a few frogs along the way. Been there, done that.

As I looked for my wonderful in a relationship, I went out with many people who were not right before I finally found the one who is. My goal in dating, after all, was not to find the quick fix, but to find the long-term relationship.

And with each person I dated, I came closer to figuring out what it was that I was looking for in a relationship – what kind of person I needed *to be* and *to have* to make me happy.

I am looking for the same in my pursuit of my professional wonderful.

I recognize that in building my business, I may need to take some work along the way that is not the perfect fit. Just like my process for post-divorce dating, there are advantages to taking on imperfect work:

1- I can chalk up those jobs as experience as I get the view from all sides.
2- It helps build my network and my portfolio of work.
3- It helps me clarify my plan for the direction I do or do not want to take my business in.
4- It will help me fund my transition into a self-sustaining business.

In some cases, it may mean that I throw it all against the wall and see what generates business for me – and then what generates business for me that I enjoy doing.

> ***"It's okay to not like it all. You can give up certain clients if it's not who you want to work with. Get a feel for your groove – that's when your business will flourish."***
>
> – Kim Albano

To do that, I need to flirt with the idea and the execution, layout the plan and my goals.

Kim Albano suggests creating a clear vision. And to do that, especially if you're a big thinker, you need to set a one-year vision and a three- to five-year vision. Once that's done, focus on the one-year plan.

That's sound advice for just about anything in life, actually. *Envision* the future, but *focus and act* on the now. And most importantly, allow the vision to be flexible, because what you're acting on now may create reasonable shifts in your future goals and expectations.

In early 2013, feeling defeated about whether I'd ever find my Mr. Wonderful in love, I jotted the following note to myself:

You deserve… and will find:

- Someone you can be yourself around.
- Someone who adores you.
- Does not belittle.
- Not afraid to tell/show you how he feels.
- Attractive – someone I like to show off.
- Confident but not cocky.

- Serious but with a sense of humor.
- Intelligent and educated.
- Ambitious – but not at the cost of others.
- Loves my kids.
- Responsible with money but not a tightwad.
- I can't wait to see him or talk to him.
- I can see forever in his eyes.
- Good sex/passion.
- Not possessive – willing to be together or away from each other.
- Faithful.
- Honest.
- Proud to have me on his arm.
- Lives locally.
- Enjoys my sense of humor.
- Enjoys theatre and culture.
- Is serious about long-term.
- Respectful to friends and family (and me).
- Can deal with cats.

- Likes to do things other than just dinner and drinks.
- Courts me.

Have I found my Mr. Wonderful? Yes.

Does he meet all of the immediate goals that I had set above? Hell, no.

And that's perfectly fine, because there are other qualities he has that are even more important *or* qualities that I didn't know I wanted before I met him.

The same is going to be true as I work to evolve my passion into a full-time career. I fully expect my list of must-haves and the things I'm willing to be flexible on from Chapter 2 to change over time. But getting it down on paper to read and revisit (often) gets you started down the right path.

MENTOR PROFILE: Amy Brooks
Author, publisher and writing coach
VoicePenPurpose.com

As I started blogging in early 2016, I was on the lookout for anyone who would listen to what I had to share. Anyone to offer advice, comment or just take a moment to read what I had to say. I was writing about stuff that was emotionally tough for me and I needed the eyeballs on what I was writing.

I noticed one day that one of my oldest and dearest friends had joined a Facebook group for writers organized by her colleague, Amy Brooks. It seemed like the opportunity I was looking for, so I pounced.

For the next several months, I shared my blogs with the group and received regular feedback from Amy (and others) about whether my writing spoke to them.

"You've got a book in there," Amy would say to me, "What's it about?"

And my response was always the same. "I'm sure there's something there, but I don't know that I have enough in me to write an entire book."

That conversation went on for months until one day the light simply went on. I messaged Amy immediately, "I'm ready."

You see, Amy Brooks comes from a long line of teachers and continued that tradition herself, teaching English in the Baltimore City and Howard County school districts for 15 years. She grew discontent with the work she was doing and the lack of balance between her job, her children and her marriage.

Somewhere along the way, she had forgotten that her passion (her wonderful) was writing, but she was getting the nudge that maybe it was time to go back to that. No matter how many times she tried to circle away from pursuing her writing bug, she just couldn't shake it.

As of this writing, Amy has released three books, *Stuff Your (Super) Mom Forgot to Tell You*, *Stuff a (First-time) Author Needs to Know* and her latest, which she co-authored, called *Spiritual Detox for Divas*.

She offers women private and group coaching sessions to those who are ready to write their first book to boost their businesses or enhance their lives. She also launched her own publishing company, Voice.Pen.Purpose., to help first-time authors self-publish their books while retaining all rights to their work.

CHAPTER 5

Committing: When It's Time for 'The Conversation'

"There are people that will come at just the right time and they will see your value."

– Amy Brooks

Call me naïve (and maybe it's a New Jersey thing), but before I got divorced, I had never heard of having 'the conversation' with someone you were dating.

For some reason, it always came up in rather hushed tones. "You and so-and-so have been dating for a while now. Is it serious? Have you had 'the conversation'?"

"Oh my god, there's supposed to be a *conversation* to declare that you are committed to that one person?" I'd think to myself.

And then I'd say, "Well, we've been seeing each other for a few months. It's serious, but no, there's never been a *conversation*."

Even in my current relationship of three years, I don't know that we've ever had 'the conversation' to declare that we are each other's one and only, but we are committed.

And similarly, I may never have the actual conversation with myself to verbalize that I am committed to being a writer, but I know in my heart that I am.

And so, like my wish list for Mr. Wonderful, I need to set my wish list (or goals) for my professional wonderful:

You deserve… and will find (Year 1):

- Keep my current job, but continue to take on freelance work where and when it's available (and reasonable).
- Finish and publish *Pursuing My Wonderful*.
- Using social media tools like LinkedIn (especially LinkedIn), Facebook and Twitter, create publicity around the book – spread the word.
- Use the opportunity to let people know that I'm available for ghostwriting or general freelance opportunities.

- Generate $10,000 in additional revenue from freelance opportunities. *Note: This is certainly not enough money for living, but it is a low-end reasonable expectation the first time out of the gate and on top of having a full-time job. I anticipate that figure will change over time, but starting small makes this a calculated risk like Tom Paolella spoke of in Chapter 2.*
- Commit to five to 10 hours a week of writing or promoting. Network, network, network to open up new opportunities. *Admittedly, networking has never been a strong suit of mine, but I recognize that pursuing my wonderful means I am my own salesperson. To succeed, I must step out of my comfort zone and sell myself.*
- Take risks. Even if I don't think I'll get the gig, start the conversation.
- Reevaluate to see what's working/not working.

You deserve… and will find (Years 3-5):
- Leave my full-time job. That may mean getting a part-time job to supplement income or to pay for benefits, but my primary source of revenue will be writing.

- Write and publish my second (and maybe third?) book.
- Maintain a solid list of clients who require repeat business while continuing to build new business.
- Be known as the expert people are looking for to motivate them to pursue their passion.

Setting these goals is 'the conversation' you need to have as you determine whether this is a passion you are willing and able to commit to. These goals should also help you determine if you need to take more of a toe-in-the-water or calculated approach instead.

Remember, your mental *and* financial well-being are at stake here.

Your goals need to be realistic enough to be achievable, but large enough to push you to successfully reach them. And success breeds more success.

"Starting businesses isn't a big deal for me. That's what I do. Starting <u>this</u> business [as an investigative medium] was extremely difficult because I'd never done it before, but I had to figure out a way to make it work."

– Laine Crosby

Setting your goals does not make the pursuit of wonderful any less daunting. As I've mentioned (several times actually) throughout this process, I have repeatedly thrown my arms up in the air and wanted to give up. It's easy to fall into that trap.

But don't.

Information and support is all around you.

> ***"One week after I had my moment of clarity, I had a logo, a tax ID and a Web site. I figured it all out by Googling it."***
>
> – Tom Paolella

No, the Internet doesn't make pursuing your passion *easy*, but it does make it *easier* simply by making practical and competitive information and communications tools available at your fingertips.

For creating my business, there is little out there today that will promote my success (and keep me on track) quite as much as my social network.

It was once written that the whole world is connected by six degrees of separation. These days, social networks like LinkedIn, Facebook and Twitter have helped dwindle the number of degrees between us and the rest of the world significantly. (In February 2016, Facebook reported their findings on the subject, citing the number as closer to 3.5 degrees.)

Regardless of where your passion brings you, if done right, this immensely valuable social currency is likely to help you find clients, partners, funding, new ideas and new resources.

> *"I started doing my investigative medium work 10 years ago. Once I built up a core base of followers, it just continued to grow and grow. It was success by grass roots."*
>
> – Laine Crosby

In other words, courting your network is as important as courting your ideas.

But with any relationship, you need to make sure you're keeping the passion alive – for you and for the people you are trying to woo once you've found the right fit.

MENTOR PROFILE:
Mark Devenpeck
Co-Founder, Triad Yoga and Pilates
TriadYogaCA.com

My relationship with Mark Devenpeck goes back 22 years (whoa, that was hard to say). I was a senior at Ithaca College and he was a freshman. I was the VP of Communications for the Student Government Association and he served as a freshman councilman. To me, he was a little brother.

Mark graduated from Ithaca with a degree in Economics and minors in both dance and audio production.

While attending Ithaca, he started receiving monthly acupuncture treatments for a fractured vertebra through the school's Chiropractic, Physical Therapy and Massage program, where he learned to heal the body without invasive surgery. At that time, his first ballet teacher at Ithaca, Eugenia Wacker-Hoeflin, also introduced him to the Alexander Technique, which helps rid the body of harmful tension.

Mark spent some time in New York City at a major record label and then moved to Philadelphia where he worked as a business manager for the telecommunications side of the business. In Philadelphia, he met Toni Zuper, a healer and body worker who would become his mentor.

Mark began his yoga training with Joel Pier from Philadelphia, a graduate of the Bikram's Yoga College of India, and then continued his education at the New York Open Center where he studied aromatherapy and became certified in Thai Yoga.

Despite his success in Philadelphia, he felt in his heart that he was not where he wanted to be. He found himself at a crossroads, with his passion for dance and a move to California lingering in the back of his mind.

"If you want to pursue dance, do it now. Otherwise, it will just become your hobby," Mark's dance company instructor, Janaea Rose Lyn, told him.

By October of 2000, Mark turned that dream into a reality, moving to California and continuing his training in dance after auditioning and being accepted at California State Long Beach. It was there that he continued his training in the holistic arts.

Prior to graduating from Cal State Long Beach in 2003, Mark studied with world-class instructors and choreographers including Doug Neilson, Sharon Kinney for modern, Alaine Haubert for ballet and Jayne Persch, Artistic Director/Choreographer at Jayne Persch & Co BRIAH Danse. Mark received a prestigious scholarship to the American Dance Festival at Duke University in 2002. He also studied with Jean McGregor in modern and Jim May and Alan Danielson from the Limon Dance Institute in New York City.

In September 2002, Mark combined his background in business with his passion for health and movement and cofounded Triad Yoga and Pilates with Newton Campbell.

Now fourteen years into their business, not only is Triad Yoga & Pilates a lasting success, but Mark's own success in dance, yoga and healing is vast and impressive.

Since opening Triad Yoga and Pilates, Mark has continued his studies, training and teaching. He went on to earn his Pilates certification from Long Beach Dance Conditioning and did additional training at California State University at Long Beach. In 2004, he went to the Omega Institute, the largest holistic studies center in the world and trained with Manju Jois. He spent six weeks at Mt. Madonna in Northern California to study with Baba Hari Dass. He has trained with Natasha Rizopoulos. He began teaching at the Bhakti West Yoga Festival in 2013 and continues today. In the summer of 2016, he took the Mindful Yoga for Cancer program at Duke University through their Integrative Medical department. He appreciates the wealth of knowledge he has received from Cyndi Lee from OM Yoga, Mark Whitwell from Heart of Yoga and considers them, along with Angela Farmer (whom he trained with at Kripalu), his biggest influences on his yoga practice.

CHAPTER 6

Keeping the Passion Alive

"Considering some people have been mediums their whole lives, I'm still relatively new at this, so I'm still thrilled by it all. And I hope the day never comes that I'm not."

– Laine Crosby

It's so, so easy for the daily grind to get in the way of nurturing your wonderful.

Guilty as charged. I can't tell you how many times I have taken my relationships - kids, my boyfriend, my family, my friends *and even me* - for granted.

Continuing that trend does nothing to advance your well-being or the well-being of everything and everyone you love.

These are the times when I make sure I go the extra mile to rein it all back in – a special home-cooked meal for my boyfriend, a day off with my kids to do whatever they want, a text or call to my parents, or "bffl day" with my best friend. It also means a pedicure or spa day for me – or even a day of sitting on my couch and writing.

So whereas in the past, I was chasing my wonderful (Mr. or otherwise), I'm rediscovering it now by reinventing it along the way and becoming clearer on who I am as a mother, girlfriend, friend, daughter and sister.

> ***"Reinvention is healthy. If you feel it's time to reinvent, it's because you've become clearer on your goals."***
>
> *– Kim Albano*

Your professional wonderful also needs this kind of TLC to keep the passion alive.

That's easy enough to do for your personal wonderful, but how can you get that spark back with your professional wonderful?

Sometimes, it's a matter of delving into what you know is working and not working and making those adjustments along the way. Other times, though, it's a matter of giving yourself some fresh perspective:

1- Celebrate the Little Victories.
2- Flirt With New Ways to Sell Yourself.
3- Practice!
4- Give Yourself Some Breathing Room.
5- Have More Intentional Conversations.
6- Cut Yourself Some Slack.
7- Lose Some Sleep Over It.

Celebrate the Little Victories

Little victories come in all shapes and sizes. Publishing my first book is a win, no doubt. But what about getting through a chapter that I found particularly difficult? What about finally settling on the title after all this work? Those were my little victories - the milestones - that kept the passion alive.

For you, your grand opening may be your main reason to celebrate, but don't lose sight of the sense of pride you felt (or will feel) when the press release you sent to the local newspaper finally gets picked up and published or when your first ad runs on the radio.

Celebrating the little victories are the butterflies in your stomach and the fluttering in your heart that scream, "I can't wait to spend more time on this!"

Flirt With New Ways to Sell Yourself

"If you get burnt out or feel stale, it's time to learn or do something new."

– Jaycee Gerard

Burn out happens. Lord knows that I have hit that point many times along the way while pursuing my wonderful.

There were days that I just sat in front of my computer staring at it and waiting for the words to start flowing. At those points, I knew that it was ineffective torture to continue sitting in front of my laptop, so I diverted my attention elsewhere.

Case in point. In formulating the final chapters of this book, I hit a point in which my only forward-moving direction was filling in gaps in content where I thought I needed it, but that wasn't bringing me any closer to completing my mission.

All of a sudden, though, a discussion about book covers and different promotional ideas breathed new life into my efforts. Simply shifting my focus to another part of my business made the whole picture a bit clearer. And once I saw *that* vision through, I was able to return to the writing end of the business a newly focused woman.

Practice!

By this point in life, we have all heard ad nauseam that "practice makes perfect," but I don't think that statement even gives practice enough credit.

> ***"Every time I practice who I am and what I stand for, I get so much more business."***
>
> – Amy Brooks

When it comes to keeping that spark alive, *practice* is the reminder to yourself and others that you are *really good* at what you do. It is the reminder that you are passionate enough about something that you are going to keep doing it and that those around you should keep paying attention.

So, don't reserve your practice for a quiet room without an audience. Go big! Practice in front of others – in person, on social media, wherever.

> ***"Build that muscle to find your voice, your confidence, your stage presence."***
>
> – Laura Virili

Amy Brooks, Laine Crosby and Laura Virili, for example, all build that muscle by way of things like podcasts, webinars or in-person public engagements. These types of efforts remind potential clients – and even yourself – that you're passionate about what you do. And that you're good at it.

Breathing Room

One of the reasons relationships didn't seem to work for me when I was first pursuing Mr. Wonderful was because I am a person who absolutely needs space. Breathing room.

That's a hard pill for some to swallow because needing space often translates to "I just don't want to be around you." It can send out a bad signal. But that wasn't actually the case.

For me, my space is my time to recharge. Alone. And without that, I am not good to anyone – not myself, my kids, my work or my Mr. Wonderful.

It should come as no surprise, then, that keeping the passion alive with my professional wonderful should also require some breathing room.

I'm not going to lie. Even in writing this book, I would put a few days of space between writing sessions. It gave me time to miss it. It gave me time to think about where I wanted to go with it.

It recharged me to the point that the next time I sat down at the computer, I would dive in head first and just start clacking away at the keys for hours at a time.

Pursuing your wonderful is going to be frustrating. It's going to have its roadblocks. And it's certainly going to have those days when you just don't want to be around it. That's okay.

Breathe. Recharge. Reignite.

Intentional Conversations

In Chapter 2, I wrote about Kim Albano's suggestion to have intentional conversations to create your business and your plan. It can also be the key to keeping the passion alive with any wonderful (or, let's be honest, even the not-so-wonderful) in your life.

Kim frequently has these intentional conversations with me – and although I have never asked, I can say with 100% certainty that I'm not the only one with whom she does this.

It's not uncommon, for example, for Kim to reach out to me when she sees that I've commented on something on her Kicking Ass & Looking Pretty Facebook page. Almost as soon as she reads it, she sends me a private message to ask for additional information or thoughts because she's thinking through the next phases of her business.

I should add that Kim's approach here is brilliant because not only does it reignite the passion she has for *her* wonderful, but it's a very subtle way of telling me (and everyone who follows her) that she's paying attention and that we are valuable to her as well. In other words, it also reignites *my* passion for *her* wonderful.

Cut Yourself Some Slack

I am my own worst critic. No one cuts me down for making a mistake or going in the wrong direction more than I do.

But the plain and simple truth is that pursuing any wonderful is going to come with hiccups and mistakes along the way – sometimes lots of them.

Don't let these mistakes stop you from moving forward with your wonderful. As I said in Chapter 3, "Stop is not a direction." Stop is simply a point that allows you to reevaluate your next steps.

Know that those challenges will be there. Prepare for them. But don't dwell on them.

Lose Some Sleep Over It (in a Good Way)

It was 4:13 a.m. when I wrote this chapter. I actually awoke at 2:00 thinking about *Pursuing My Wonderful* and things I wanted to add or finesse. I tried to push it all away and go back to sleep, but by 3:00 a.m. I knew that was pointless, so I ran downstairs and grabbed my laptop. I knew I'd probably regret that decision later and would likely have to fight nodding off at my full-time job, but the pull-me-out-of-bed excitement is sometimes the renewal you need.

The passion in any relationship comes and goes. That's normal. But if it's the right fit – the prince and not the frog, if you will – then it's worth going through the steps to reignite the passion as long as it's necessary.

MENTOR PROFILE: Jaycee Gerard
Photographer
JayceeGerardPhoto.com

"If you really want someone who's good with styling thin hair, you should go to this guy at South Street Salon," my best friend suggested.

That was in 2008, when I was on the edge of divorce and needed to be reminded that I was beautiful inside and out. I jumped on that opportunity and was thrilled to have a stylist who was so passionate about his job.

Like any stylist/client relationship begins, we talked about what I wanted to do with my hair and then moved on to conversations about our kids, our lives, things we liked and didn't like. During the conversation, I noticed a bag of photography equipment at his station.

"Oh, I see you do photography," I commented.

And just when you think someone's eyes couldn't light up any more about the job they were already doing, his eyes grew even brighter.

"When my daughter was born in 2008, my mother bought us this camera," he said, "It sat on top of the refrigerator most of the time, and I'd pull it down to take pictures every now and then using the auto settings. And then one day, I started paying attention to all the buttons and wanted to learn about what they did."

Jaycee was teaching himself all he could about photography and regaled me with everything he was learning about the trade- and picking up information and tricks of the trade with anyone who was willing to sit down and speak with him about it.

In the eight years since then, I have watched Jaycee turn his second passion into a successful part-time business, shooting weddings and portraits for families across the Jersey Shore area – including my headshot for this book.

CHAPTER 7

SURVIVING 'THE LOVERS' QUARREL'

L et's face it. Even if you're taking all the right steps to court your wonderful and keep the passion alive once you've made the commitment, it will not always be rainbows and unicorns.

This is true of love. This is true of family. This is true of your career.

There will undoubtedly be times when your wonderful, the thing that normally brings you so much joy, turns on you and you're left questioning whether you've made the right life choices.

In these times of woe, *don't* act in haste. All relationships (even with your professional wonderful) are a work in progress and you must never treat them as anything else.

As you build your business, these 'lovers' quarrels' can appear in a few ways:

1- The conflict within.

2- The client dispute.

3- The domestic dispute.

And none of these quarrels signal the end. They signal opportunity.

The Conflict Within

If you have started your business on your own, your 'lovers' quarrel' may be strictly between you and your passion. The internal conflict with your wonderful may feel insurmountable and one-sided, but that doesn't mean it can't be resolved.

In your romantic relationships, haven't there been times when you've beaten yourself up because you *perceive* that you aren't giving 100% as a girlfriend or wife?

Or from a different angle, haven't there been times when, as a mother, you have questioned whether or not you're doing the job right - when you dwell on how a decision you have made is going to impact your child in the long run?

Regardless of how many times you ever felt this way, you have likely never quit being a girlfriend or wife because of those feelings. You've never quit being a mother.

The same is true of your professional wonderful – with similar ways to resolve the issue(s).

First, take a breath. Step away and give yourself a little distance from the naysayer within.

Identify what isn't working for you and then take the time to reinvent.

Remember, reinvention is not failure. Rather, as Kim Albano said in Chapter 6, it's done in a moment when you have a little more clarity on what your vision is.

Have more intentional conversations if it suits you – anything to clear your mind and get you back on the right path to being happy with your professional wonderful.

The Client Dispute

The client dispute is sometimes a little more difficult to *want* to fix because, while you are committed to your business, you have the freedom to choose with whom you wish to work. In other words, it may be pretty darn tempting to just get up and walk away all together.

But remember, these people help pay the bills and,

probably even more importantly, they are the grass roots of your future success.

Difficult customers or clients happen, but each and every one of them offers a teaching moment, even if you're not particularly fond of what they have to say or how they're expressing it. Use their issues and concerns to your advantage as you build up your professional wonderful. So, take a deep breath and:

1. Practice being an active (and intentional) listener. Pay attention to client concerns and try to address them proactively moving forward.
2. Begin to redefine your target client/audience if necessary.
3. Identify preferred communications methods to help manage client expectations and eliminate some back and forth moving forward.
4. Get the job done. Unless you are dealing with an extreme situation where you or your business are being threatened or harmed, puff up your chest and finish the job. It will feel like a big win for you in the long run even if it doesn't feel that way when you're in the moment.

The Domestic Dispute

If you have partners or employees, you know that you spend more time with these people than you do your loved ones. Sometimes they even are your loved ones.

And though you may have had multi-year relationships with any or all of the people who work with you, it does not mean that working side-by-side will necessarily have a natural flow – especially not right off the bat. No doubt, this can cause some tremendous rifts between individuals, especially where shared financial responsibility is involved.

Even if you think you've thought it all through and have it sorted out before working together, there are going to be issues (new or recurring) that will require honest conversations to determine how best to handle the situation in the event that it comes up again.

"We struggled in the beginning with who was responsible for what. But we soon realized that he was the guy who looked at bottom line, and I looked at the big picture. Once we figured that out, it got a lot easier."

– Mark Devenpeck

My Mr. Wonderful and I do not live together, but we spend an awful lot of time together in the evenings and on the weekends. And after three years, I have learned that he is a bit more (okay, far more) fastidious than I am about cleanliness and organization. For example, I know that he hates how my fridge is organized (or rather the lack of organization). So after a trip to the grocery store, it's not uncommon that he will pull apart a six pack of drinks and organize them rather than leaving them bundled.

I'm not going to lie, this used to make my blood boil because that simply was not how *I* did things. I realize now, though, that it's such a little thing that if it makes him feel better to do it his way, it's not a battle worth fighting. It's really no big deal. And he's better at it than I am.

It is the same way with a business partnership. Pick your battles. And figure out who's best at doing what.

After all, there are reasons why big corporations hire people for specific roles – it's because people have different levels of expertise in different areas – and they've hired them specifically to make the business succeed in that space.

More Than Just a 'Lovers' Quarrel'

Presumably, the professional wonderful you have created has a pretty solid foundation – you enjoy it, you can monetize it and you can grow it. And I would rarely suggest abandoning ship altogether.

However…

Staying in any relationship simply because it feels like it's the best you will ever do serves no purpose for you.

If your wonderful and the decisions you have to make for it to last hurts you physically, emotionally or financially, get out. Move on.

CHAPTER 8

PURSUE YOUR WONDERFUL

That feeling in your gut? That's your wonderful trying to make itself known.

Maybe you've just started feeling it or maybe it's been that tiny tickle inside that you've been feeling for years. Don't deny it. Don't doubt yourself.

Go on. Pursue your wonderful.

"Your life experience already makes you an expert."

– Laura Virili

Need help? Try some of the exercises I went through as I pursued my wonderful!

Exercise 1: What does your wonderful look like?

_____

_____

_____

_____

_____

Exercise 2: What are the pros and cons of pursuing your professional wonderful?

Pros:	**Cons:**

Exercise 3: What are you flexible on and what are your must-haves?

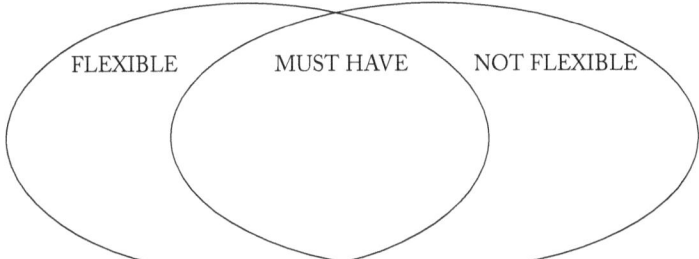

Exercise 4: What is at the cross-section of what you're good at and what you love?

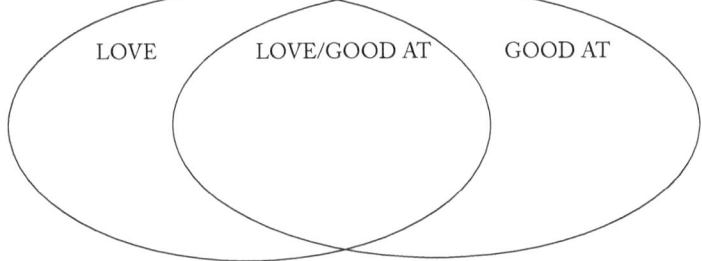

Exercise 5: What does your wonderful have to offer that others may not already be offering?

_____

_____

_____

_____

_____

Exercise 6: What are the outside boundaries of your wonderful?

_____

_____

_____

_____

_____

_____

_____

Exercise 7: What does your wonderful look like in years one to three?

_____

_____

_____

_____

_____

_____

_____

Exercise 8: What does your wonderful look like in years three to five?

_____

_____

_____

_____

_____

_____

_____

Exercise 9: Who are the people in your physical and social networks who can you see your wonderful through?

_____

_____

_____

_____

_____

_____

_____

Exercise 10: How will you keep the spark in your wonderful alive?

_____

_____

_____

_____

_____

_____

_____

Acknowledgements

In weirdly appropriate timing, as I wind down the writing of *Pursuing My Wonderful*, I have *It's a Wonderful Life* playing on the television in the background. Those who know me would not be at all surprised that the end of this movie has me in tears.

There are two things in the final scene that really hurl me over the emotional edge:

The inscription in Clarence's copy of *Tom Sawyer*: *"Remember, George no man is a failure who has friends."*

and

"A toast to my big brother, George: The richest man in town."

So with that, I would like to offer a huge thank you to those who have made me both rich and successful regardless of where my journey to pursue my wonderful brings me.

To Nick and Chris, you have always been my best cheerleaders, my biggest supporters. You know this has been my dream for almost as long as you've been in my life. Thank you for believing me! I truly could not have asked for better children and I love you so much. I promise to encourage you to pursue your wonderful when it's time for you to make your big life decisions.

To Mom and Dad who said, "It's about time," when I told them I was writing a book. Thank you so much for all you have given me in life, not the least of which has been your love and support through my many, many ups and downs.

To Heather, I don't know where to begin. You've listened to me laugh and cry through every big (and small) life event and maintained a fine balance of listening and offering advice for more than 40 years. Thank goodness for that. Thank you also for you, Mike, Jackie and Iain playing such a big part in the lives of me and the boys.

To John and Lexi, my Mr. Wonderful and my 'bffl,' you have been the greatest additions to my life in my adult years and have helped me believe in who I am and stand up for what's good for me.

To Laura, Kim, Amy, Laine, Mark, Tom and Jaycee,

thank you for being my inspiration and sharing your own magical words and encouragement to get this book out there.

There have been so many people in my life who have been there to support me and encourage me through every single stage of my life. I see you. And your contributions have been invaluable.

ABOUT THE AUTHOR

Beth Tancredi won her first creative writing award in the third grade (Thank you, Mrs. Larsen!) for a short children's story called, "A Pet for Me." The book scored her a seat at the Young Author's Conference in Connecticut and opened her up to a lifelong love of writing.

Following her graduation from Ithaca College, she retired her creative pen to start her career. She has spent the last 20 years working in broadcast, print and digital media, financial services and health care.

Now, she has picked up her pen again (keyboard, actually) to follow her dreams of being an author, writing for herself and others.

Beth has two children, Nick and Chris, and is a long-time resident of the Jersey Shore.

Email: contact@bethtancredi.com
Twitter: @bethtancredi
Website: bethtancredi.com

www.ingramcontent.com/pod-product-compliance
Lightning Source LLC
Chambersburg PA
CBHW071301040426
42444CB00009B/1813